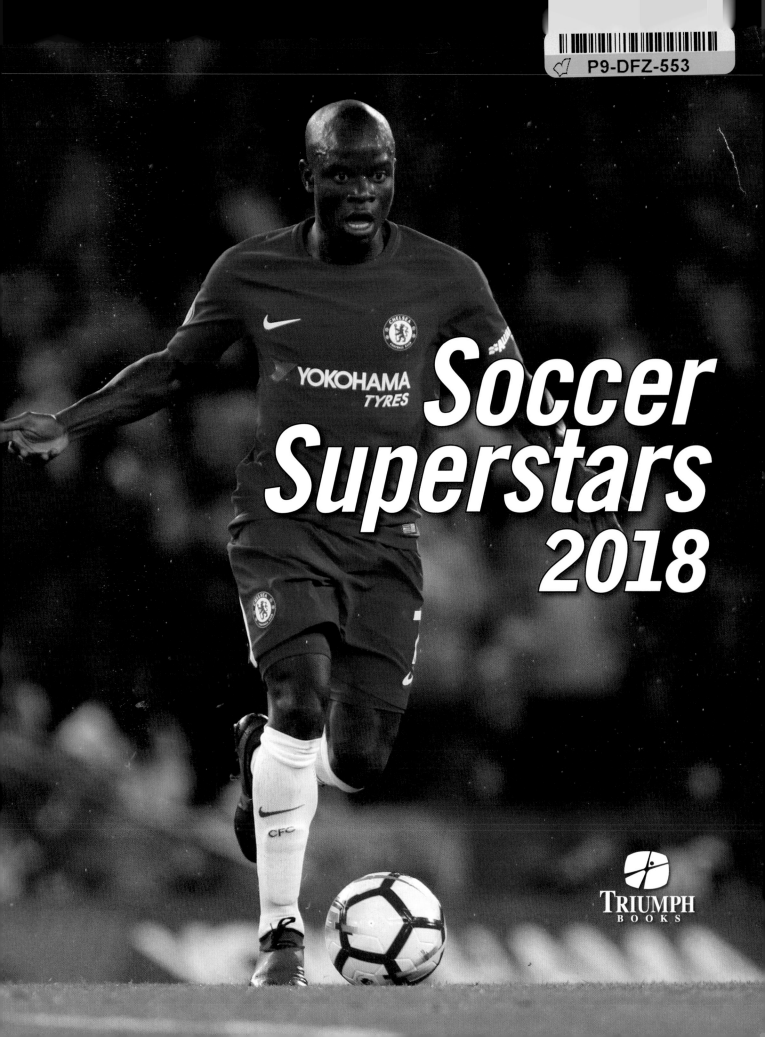

Soccer Superstars 2018

TRIUMPH
BOOKS

Triumph Books LLC
814 North Franklin Street
Chicago, Illinois, 60610
Phone: (312) 337-0747
www.triumphbooks.com

Printed in the United States of America

ISBN: 978-1-62937-574-8

All photos courtesy of AP Images

Contents

Neymar

Hometown: São Paulo, Brazil
Club: Paris Saint-Germain

N eymar da Silva Santos Jr. drew attention for his stunning soccer skills from an early age in football-crazed Brazil. Joining the youth academy of Santos FC at 11, he was already being courted by European powerhouse Real Madrid at 14. Santos convinced him to stay in Brazil, however, and soon he would star for the senior club.

Neymar made his professional debut for Santos in 2009, scoring 14 goals in 48 games. Over the next four seasons, he would become a star, scoring 122 goals for Santos and earning numerous awards, including South American Footballer of the Year in 2011 and 2012. He would also contribute 46 goals for the Brazil national team in 67 caps and help lead Brazil to the final of the 2012 Olympics against Mexico. In the summer of 2013, he spurred Brazil to victory in the Confederations Cup, scoring a goal in the final versus Spain and being named MVP of the Tournament.

It was just after defeating Spain with his countrymen that Neymar moved across the Atlantic to join Barcelona. In his first season with the star-stacked club, he scored 15 goals in 41 matches. But it was his 2014–2015 season in which he truly broke out, scoring 39 goals, second on Barça only to Lionel Messi. He was the top scorer in the Copa del Rey with seven goals and tied Messi and Cristiano Ronaldo as top goalscorer in the Champions League with 10, both of which Barcelona won. He also played brilliantly for Brazil in the 2014 World Cup before a back injury derailed their run. A dazzling ball-handler and especially lethal on free kicks, Neymar has explosive scoring ability from anywhere on the pitch.

In August 2017, Neymar moved to Paris Saint-Germain for a record $263 million fee and a five-year contract that made him the highest-paid soccer player in the world.

Fast Stat:

105

Number of goals Neymar scored in four seasons with FC Barcelona

Ht: 5'9" • **Wt:** 150 • **DOB:** 2/5/92

Position: Forward/Winger

2017–2018 salary:
$53 million

Career club goals/International caps:
249 goals/81 caps

Twitter: @neymarjr

Did you know? His father, Neymar Santos Sr., was also a professional soccer player.

As a kid: Neymar enjoyed playing street football and futsal, a version of indoor soccer.

Favorite foods: Italian, Japanese

Hobbies: Wakeboarding, dancing, and music

Favorite music: Brazilian music, particularly Música sertaneja

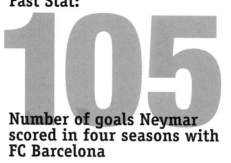

> *"I think...Neymar will become the top goalscorer in Brazil's history, surpassing Pelé."*
>
> —Brazil legend Romário

Toni Kroos

Hometown:
Greifswalder, Germany
Club: Real Madrid

2

Number of clubs with whom Toni has won a Champions League title, the first German player ever to do it

Ht: 6'0" • **Wt:** 172 • **DOB:** 1/4/90

Position: Midfield

2017–2018 salary:
$23.7 million

Career club goals/International caps:
47 goals/79 caps

Twitter: @ToniKroos

Did you know? Toni's younger brother Felix plays midfield for second-division Bundesliga team Union Berlin.

As a kid: A prodigy in soccer, Toni was not the best student in school—perhaps because he missed up to 40 days a year training at soccer.

Favorite foods: Healthy foods rich in protein and carbs, rarely junk food

Hobbies: Playing with his dogs, tennis, and poker

Favorite music: German classic rock

Born in the former East Germany, Toni Kroos has the unique distinction of being the only World Cup winner born in the former Soviet satellite. Shortlisted for FIFA's Golden Ball award for the tournament's best player, Kroos scored twice in two minutes in Germany's shocking 7–1 upset seminfinal win over host Brazil and was named man of the match. He also led the tournament in assists and rated as its top player according to the Castrol Performance Index. His standout role in Germany's 2014 World Cup run earned him an offer he couldn't refuse from Real Madrid later that summer, leading him to leave Bayern Munich and the Bundesliga for Spanish La Liga.

A prototypical attacking midfielder, Kroos is known for his vision, passing accuracy, and ability to set up scoring opportunities for teammates. Coming up through his local club team as a youth, Kroos transferred to Bayern Munich's youth program at 16. A year later, in 2007, he was promoted to the senior team, making him the youngest player at the time to ever appear for Bayern in a match, at 17 years, eight months, and two days old. Though Bayern loaned Kroos to rival Bayer Leverkusen for 18 months, he would spend almost five seasons with Munich, becoming one of the best players in Europe, and helping the Bavarians to three league championships, three DFB-Pokal cups, and a Champions League title in 2012–2013.

Since joining Real Madrid, Kroos has gone on to help the Blancos win a UEFA Super Cup, a FIFA Club World Cup, and another Champions League title, while being named to the Champions League Squad of the Season four straight years.

"How Toni distributes the ball, how he receives it, is very good. He's technically excellent."

—Joachim Löw,
manager of the German national team

N'Golo Kanté

Hometown: Paris, France
Club: Chelsea

From obscurity in the third division of French soccer in 2013, N'Golo Kanté has risen farther and faster than just about any other footballer on the planet. The catalyst on a Leicester City team that shocked England and the world by winning its first ever Premier League title in 2016, N'Golo was named Leicester City's Players' Player of the Year. Signing with Chelsea for the 2016–2017 season, N'Golo again led his team to the league championship and this time was named the PFA Players' Player of the Year, the Premier League Player of the Season, and the FWA Footballer of the Year.

Underestimated from an early age due to his small stature, N'Golo's ability, energy, and work ethic have made him one of the top defenders and most valuable players in the world. In his breakout season with Leicester, N'Golo led the Premier League in tackles (175) and interceptions (157)—both by a wide margin. And when he departed for Chelsea (the only Leicester player who left that year), his old team fell off precipitously, while his new team won the league title. Twice with Chelsea, N'Golo has been named Man of the Match—once in a 3–0 win against his former team and again in a March 2017 1–0 victory over Man United in which he scored the only goal. *L'Équipe* named him the world's sixth-best footballer of 2016, and he was nominated for the Ballon d'Or in 2017.

Born in Paris to Malian immigrants, N'Golo decided to play for France and debuted on the senior side in 2016, making his first start and scoring his first goal on his 25th birthday against Russia. He plans to join Antoine Griezmann and Paul Pogba on a loaded French squad and make a serious run at World Cup glory in 2018.

Fast Stat:

175

Number of tackles N'Golo made in 2015–2016 for Leicester, 31 more than any other Premier League player

Ht: 5'6" • **Wt:** 150 • **DOB:** 3/29/91

Position: Midfield

2017–2018 salary: $8.2 million

Career club goals/International caps: 14 club goals/20 caps

Twitter: @nglkante

Did you know? N'Golo passed his qualification in accountancy when he was 20 in case the whole soccer thing didn't pan out.

Fun tidbit: The Twitter account @KanteFacts posts "facts" about N'Golo, like, "70% of the Earth is covered by water. The rest is covered by Ngolo Kante."

As a kid: Although N'Golo has been compared to Claude Makélélé, his role model growing up was Lassana Diarra, whom he replaced in his debut with France in a friendly versus the Netherlands for his first cap.

> *"Kanté is by far the best player in the league."*
>
> —Alex Ferguson

Marco Reus

Hometown: Dortmund, Germany
Club: Borussia Dortmund

Known for his speed, versatility, and technique, Marco Reus has become an offensive star of the Bundesliga, where he has spent his club career, and since 2010 as a member and then starter for the eventual World Cup–champion German national team.

Joining the youth program of his hometown Borussia Dortmund club at the age of seven, Reus spent 10 years coming up through Dortmund's ranks. But Dortmund let him go in 2006 to play for the U-19 team of Rot Weiss Ahlen, where he broke into the first team within a year. By 2008–2009 he was a mainstay, playing in 27 matches and scoring four goals. This led to his signing with Bundesliga club Borussia Mönchengladbach, where he would become a prolific goalscorer, netting 41 goals over three seasons. At the end of the 2011–2012 season, Reus was named the Footballer of the Year in Germany. His old club took notice.

Signing Reus away for a $19.6 million transfer fee, Borussia Dortmund reclaimed the hometown midfielder before the start of the 2012–2013 season. He scored a goal in his August debut with Dortmund and then two more for a brace against his former team in September. Reus and teammate Mario Götze soon became one of the most dangerous midfield duos in soccer, until Götze left for Bayern Munich in 2013. Reus has scored 62 goals with Dortmund since rejoining the team, including six in his first six games of 2015. He has helped Dortmund to two DFL-Supercups and was named the Dortmund Player of the Year for 2013–2014 as well as being named to the Champions League Team of the Season.

Fast Stat:

89

Goals scored by Marco in his first five seasons with Borussia Dortmund

Ht: 5'11" • **Wt:** 165 • **DOB:** 5/31/89

Position: Midfield/Winger

2017–2018 salary:
$4.7 million

Career club goals/International caps:
136 goals/29 caps

Twitter: @woodyinho

Did you know? German newspaper *Bild* nicknamed Marco "Rolls Reus."

Fun tidbit: One of the tattoos on Marco's left arm is a quote by Oprah, which reads, "The biggest adventure you can take is to live your Dreams."

As a kid: Marco began playing for his hometown club Post SV Dortmund at the age of five.

Favorite foods: Mashed potatoes, goulash, and cabbage

Hobbies: Ping-Pong and video games (especially EA Sport's FIFA series)

Favorite music: R&B and hip-hop, Lena, and Justin Bieber

*"My idol was always Tomáš Rosický...
I copied everything about him, right
down to his sweatbands."*

—Marco Reus on the former Dortmund midfielder

"Agüero is every bit as important to [Man City] as Luis Suárez was to Liverpool last year or Gareth Bale to Tottenham Hotspur the year before."

—English soccer journalist Martin Samuel

Sergio Agüero

Hometown:
Buenos Aires, Argentina
Club: Manchester City

Known to all by his nickname "Kun," Agüero has been compared to Brazilian soccer legend Romário, as well as his former father-in-law, Diego Maradona. After scoring five goals for Man City in just 20 minutes in a match against Newcastle early in the 2015–2016 season, there may soon be no one left to compare Kun to.

Raised in modest circumstances, Agüero became the youngest player to appear in a match for Independiente at the age of 15 in 2003. In 2005–2006 he scored 18 goals in just 36 games and was quickly scooped up by La Liga club Atlético Madrid, where he spent five seasons, quickly becoming Atlético's top offensive threat, scoring 101 goals in 234 matches.

Agüero joined Manchester City in 2011 for a Sky Blues record transfer fee of £35 million. His impact was felt immediately, as he shined in his debut, scoring an assist and two goals. But it was in the final match of the season that Agüero became a local legend. His goal in the 95th minute gave Man City its first Premier League title and its first top-division trophy since 1968. City of Manchester Stadium erupted as Agüero's teammates mobbed him on the field. Another league title followed in 2013–2014, along with a League Cup.

Agüero won a Gold Medal with Argentina in the 2008 Olympics. Teamed with Lionel Messi again for the 2014 World Cup, Argentina finished as runners-up to Germany. A young, stout striker who plays with strength, agility, and speed, Kun Agüero looks to be getting better and should be a force for years to come.

Fast Stat:

5

Goals Kun scored in 20 minutes vs. Newcastle on October 3, 2015

Ht: 5′8″ • **Wt:** 170 • **DOB:** 6/2/88

Position: Striker

2017–2018 salary:
$15 million

Career goals/International caps:
301 goals/82 caps

Personal homepage:
www.sergioaguero.com/EN

Twitter: @aguerosergiokun

Did you know? A tattoo on Kun's right arm is written in Elvish, the Middle Earth language J.R.R. Tolkien invented for *The Lord of the Rings*.

As a kid: He liked to repeat the name "Kum Kum" from his favorite cartoon (as "Kun Kun"), so a family friend dubbed him "Kun."

Favorite foods: Argentine beef and pasta (both of which Kun had to cut from his diet to avoid injury)

Hobbies: Making defenders look foolish and hanging with Argentina national teammate Lionel Messi

Favorite music: Cumbia (Kun sang on Los Leales' song "El Kun Agüero")

Cristiano Ronaldo

Hometown:
Funchal, Madeira, Portugal
Club: Real Madrid

Fast Stat:

6

Number of consecutive seasons with 50 or more goals, an unmatched record

If the best soccer player in the world isn't Lionel Messi, it has to be Cristiano Ronaldo, the Portuguese superstar who spent six seasons with Manchester United before joining Real Madrid, the archrival of Messi's Barcelona club. Winning the Ballon d'Or in 2014 and 2016 and the Best FIFA Men's Player of 2017, Ronaldo has made the case over the last few years that he, not Messi, is the best player of his generation.

What isn't debatable is Ronaldo's claim as being one of the greatest footballers in the history of the sport. His professional career began at the age of 16 with Sporting CP in Lisbon, where he became the only player to ever advance from the under-16 team to first team in one season. It didn't take long for English powerhouse Manchester United to take notice, and they signed Ronaldo for £12.24 million in 2003.

Given the No. 7 shirt worn by David Beckham, Ronaldo quickly lived up to expectations. During 2007–2008, he scored 31 goals for Man U, helping his team to their second of three straight Premier League championships and his first Ballon d'Or. Ronaldo also excelled for the Portugal national team, being named permanent captain in July 2008 and helping Portugal to the UEFA Euro 2016 championship.

Moving to his current team, Real Madrid, in 2009, Ronaldo became its leading goalscorer of all-time in only six-plus seasons and led Madrid to a league title in 2011–2012 and in 2016–2017. In 2016 he led his Portugal national team to victory over France in the UEFA European Championship and won his fifth Ballon d'Or, tying Lionel Messi for most all-time.

Ht: 6'1" • **Wt:** 180 • **DOB:** 2/5/85

Position: Forward

2017–2018 salary: $35.9 million

Career club goals/International caps: 536 goals/147 caps

Personal homepage: www.cristianoronaldo.com

Twitter: @Cristiano

Did you know? At 15 Ronaldo was diagnosed with a career-threatening heart condition that required surgery to repair.

As a kid: Ronaldo grew up on the island of Madeira, where at the age of eight he joined the amateur team Andorinha, where his father was the kit man.

Fun tidbit: Ronaldo, who goes by his second given name, was named after Ronald Reagan, his father's favorite actor.

Favorite foods: Bacalhau à Brás (a traditional Portuguese dish of salted cod, potatoes, onions, and eggs)

Hobbies: Cars, fashion, and charity

Favorite music: Elton John, Phil Collins, and Brazilian music

"If Messi is the best on the planet, Ronaldo is the best in the universe."

—Former Real Madrid manager
José Mourinho

Lionel Messi

Hometown: Rosario, Argentina
Club: FC Barcelona

Fast Stat:

91

Record number of goals Leo scored for Barcelona and Argentina in 2012

Ht: 5′6″ • **Wt:** 148 • **DOB:** 6/24/87

Position: Striker

2017–2018 salary:
$44.9 million

Career club goals/International caps:
533 goals/122 caps

Twitter: @_10_lionelmessi

Did you know? Leo is left-footed, and most of his goals are struck by his prodigious left foot.

As a kid: From the age of six to 12, Leo scored nearly 500 goals for Newell's Old Boys, his youth team in Rosario, Argentina.

Favorite foods: Milanesa Napolitana

Hobbies: Playing guitar and spending time with his partner, Antonella Roccuzzo, and their two sons, Thiago and Mateo

Favorite music: Cumbia, reggae

Bursting onto the international soccer scene in 2004 as a 17-year-old, Leo Messi's status as one of the world's top two footballers is unquestioned. The only question remaining for the player often compared to Pelé and fellow Argentinian Diego Maradona, is whether he will surpass (or has already surpassed) those two legends.

At the age of 11, a growth hormone deficiency nearly derailed his career, but an offer from FC Barcelona to cover his treatments and play at their youth academy in 2000 brought Messi to Spain to stay. It proved to be an insanely good investment for Barcelona, as Messi soon climbed the ranks of Barça's junior teams.

Messi made his La Liga debut on October 16, 2004, and quickly became a starter and star for one of Europe's top teams, helping Barça to eight league titles in 12 seasons. Displaying unmatched ball-handling skills, Messi weaves around and often through defenders as if the ball were attached to his foot by an invisible string—until he launches it into the back of the opponents' net. The leading scorer in La Liga history, he also holds the league assist record.

In 2014–2015 Messi scored 58 goals while leading Barça to its second treble—winning La Liga, the Copa del Rey, and the Champions League in one season—while winning the UEFA Best Player in Europe award for the second time. He also captained the Argentina national team to a runner-up finish in the 2014 World Cup, where he earned the Golden Ball as the tournament's best player. Messi was the first player to win five Ballons d'Or and has also won four European Golden Shoes.

"*Messi is an alien who dedicates himself to playing with humans.*"

—Gianluigi Buffon

"[Antoine] works hard for his team and possesses technique, vision, and quality finishing."

—Ioan Lupescu,
UEFA chief technical officer

Antoine Griezmann

Hometown: Mâcon, France
Club: Atlético Madrid

Even as a child Antoine Griezmann was underestimated due to his slight stature. But between Antoine's determination and his footballing genes—his Portuguese grandfather was a professional footballer—he attracted the notice of several teams' youth programs. At 14, Spanish club Real Sociedad offered him a contract. Though it meant moving to San Sebastian, his parents agreed to let him follow his dream.

After four years on Sociedad's youth team, Antoine made his first-team debut in September 2009 and scored his first professional goal the same month. He would go on to net six goals that season, helping Sociedad to win the Segunda División and launch the team back into La Liga. Real Sociedad continued its winning ways, and in 2013 Antoine scored on a spectacular overhead kick against Lyon that helped it qualify for its second Champions League appearance and first in 10 years.

In July 2014 Antoine transferred to Atlético Madrid, one of the top teams in La Liga, and soon became one of the league's top players, scoring his first hat trick in December and being named La Liga Player of the Month for January 2015. In April 2016, he knocked Barcelona out of the Champions League with a pair of goals in a 2–0 victory and then in May scored the decisive goal to eliminate Bayern Munich. He's won a host of awards, including being named French Player of the Year in 2016 and was named to the Champions League Team of the Season in 2015–2016 and 2016–17. Antoine led the French national team to the Euro 2016 championship game (losing 1–0 to Portugal) and won both Player of the Tournament and the Golden Boot as the tournament's top scorer.

Fast Stat:

83

Goals Antoine scored in his first three seasons with Atlético Madrid

Ht: 5'9" • **Wt:** 152 • **DOB:** 3/21/91

Position: Forward

2017–2018 salary: $7.7 million

Career club goals/International caps: 138 goals/47 caps

Twitter: @AntoGriezmann

Did you know? Antoine's sister Maude survived the Paris attacks of November 2015 at the Bataclan theater, while he was playing for France against Germany at the Stade de France.

As a kid: French club Lyon rejected Antoine due to his small size and frail frame.

Fun tidbit: Antoine wears his Spongebob Squarepants underwear on game days.

Favorite foods: New York style pizza

Hobbies: Playing computer games

Favorite music: Drake, whose "Hotline Bling" video inspired his goal celebration

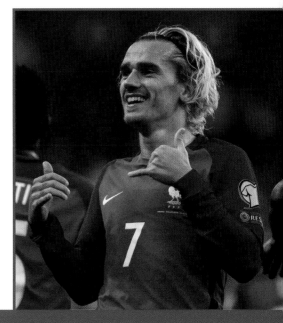

"The one who plays this game the best is Iniesta... He picks the right moment to do everything: when to dribble, when to speed things up, and when to slow things down."

—Former Argentinian great
Juan Román Riquelme

Andrés Iniesta

Hometown: Fuentealbilla, Spain
Club: FC Barcelona

One of the greatest all-around players of the last 12 years and probably one of the greatest midfielders of all-time, Barcelona captain Andrés Iniesta has been an integral part of championship squads for both Barça and Spain's national team.

Born and raised in a small village in the southeast of the Castile–La Mancha region of Spain, Iniesta was recruited at the age of 12 to join FC Barcelona's youth academy. Though homesick and shy around the older soccer prodigies, Iniesta captained Barça's Under-15 team to victory in the Nike Premier Cup in 1999. He debuted for the first team at the age of 18 in 2002, began playing regularly in 2004, and has never stopped.

Iniesta was instrumental in helping Barça to a record six trophies in 2009, the year he was named La Liga Spanish Player of the Year. A critical part of a Barcelona team that has won eight league championships, four Copa del Reys, four Champions League titles, and two FIFA Club World Cups, Iniesta has also earned numerous individual awards, including the 2014 Golden Foot and 2012 UEFA Best Player in Europe Award.

After helping its Under-16 and Under-19 teams to European Championships, Iniesta made Spain's national team in 2006. Spain won the UEFA Euro 2008 with Iniesta named to the Team of the Tournament. Then, in the 2010 World Cup, Spain reached the final against The Netherlands after three 1–0 wins. In the 116th minute of the game, Iniesta netted the game-winner to give Spain another 1–0 win and its first-ever World Championship. His entire career spent in Spain, Iniesta is without a doubt one of the best Spaniards of all-time.

Ht: 5′7″ • **Wt:** 143 • **DOB:** 5/11/84

Position: Midfield

2017–2018 salary: $11.3 million

Career club goals/International caps: 56 goals/121 caps

Twitter: @andresiniesta8

Did you know? Andrés earned a yellow card after his 2010 World Cup–winning goal for taking off his jersey, which revealed a handwritten message on his undershirt in tribute to late teammate Dani Jarque.

As a kid: Andrés' father saved for three months to be able to buy him a pair of Adidas Predator boots.

Favorite foods: Chicken with potatoes

Hobbies: Harvesting grapes at the family vineyard, listening to music, spending time with family

Favorite music: English indie rock band Kasabian and Spanish rock/rumba duo Estopa

Mesut Özil

Hometown: Gelsenkirchen, Germany
Club: Arsenal

25

Number of assists Mesut amassed for Real Madrid in 2010–2011, leading all European professionals

Ht: 5'11" • **Wt:** 168 • **DOB:** 10/15/88

Position: Midfield

2017–2018 salary:
$9.6 million

Career club goals/International caps:
78 goals/86 caps

Twitter: @MesutOzil1088

Did you know? With Arsenal's club-record transfer fee of £42.5 million, Mesut became the most expensive German footballer of all-time.

Fun Fact: Özil donated his 2014 World Cup winnings, an estimated $306,000, to pay for 23 sick Brazilian kids to have surgery as a "personal thank you for the hospitality of the people of Brazil."

As a kid: Mesut developed his soccer skills while playing with friends in the "Monkey Cage," a local field enclosed by fences.

Favorite foods: Kebabs; and ice cream, which is unfortunate as Mesut is lactose-intolerant.

Hobbies: In keeping with Mesut's uncany ability to anticipate what's going to happen on the field, his favorite game away from it is chess.

Favorite music: Rap, Wiz Khalifa

Known for his ability to set up his teammates for goalscoring opportunities, Mesut Özil broke out in the 2010 World Cup as a 21-year-old midfielder for the German national team. He was nominated for the Golden Ball, awarded to the tournament's best all-around player. Soon Real Madrid came calling, and Özil's career took off.

An attacking midfielder who tends to improvise on the pitch and play with finesse, Özil has been compared to Real Madrid legend Zinedine Zidane for his style and assist-making skills.

Of Turkish descent, Özil was born and raised in Gelsenkirchen, Germany, where he began his youth career before moving to Rot-Weiss Essen at the age of 12. In 2005 he transferred to Bundesliga mainstay Schalke 04, where he first broke onto the first team, playing two seasons there and then two years with German rival Werder Bremen.

Although he could have played for Turkey, Özil, a third-generation German, never doubted that he'd play for the country of his birth. Making the German team in 2009, he shone in Germany's 2010 third-place World Cup finish and was crucial in the team's 2014 World Cup title.

After establishing himself as a bona fide star with Real Madrid from 2010–2013—leading La Liga in assists all three seasons and being shortlisted for the Ballon D'or—Özil moved to the Premier League and Arsenal for a club-record transfer fee, where he has become an integral part of one of the top teams in the league, continuing to rack up assists, goals, and wins.

"Özil is unique. There is no copy of him—not even a bad copy."

— Former Real Madrid manager José Mourinho

"The best goalkeeper I have ever faced was Buffon....it was almost impossible to beat him!"

—Zlatan Ibrahimović

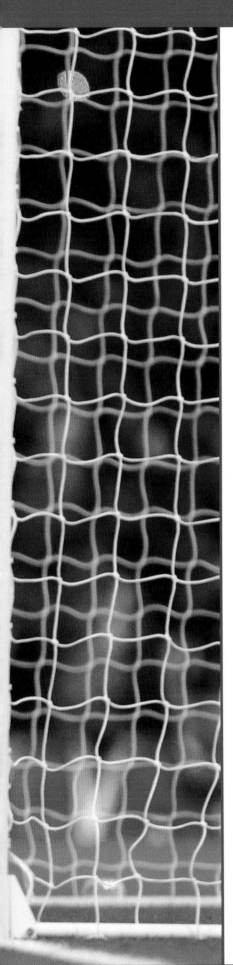

Gianluigi Buffon

Hometown: Carrara, Italy
Club: Juventus

Widely regarded as one of the greatest goalkeepers of all-time, Gianluigi "Gigi" Buffon is in the 23rd season of a career in which he's been named Serie A Goalkeeper of the Year 11 times, IFFHS World's Best Goalkeeper four times, UEFA Club Goalkeeper of the Year twice, IFFHS Best Goalkeeper of the 21st Century, won a Golden Foot, and was runner-up for the Ballon d'Or. He's also won eight Serie A titles, four Coppa Italias, and a UEFA Cup. What's perhaps most amazing for the 39-year-old keeper is that many of his best years have come in the last five seasons.

Gigi began his career at the age of 13 with Parma's youth program as a mid-fielder. Injuries to the team's top two goalkeepers led to his being inserted at goal, and within two weeks he was the youth team's No. 1 keeper. He made it to the senior squad at the age of 17 in 1995 and debuted with a clean sheet in a 0–0 draw against league champion Milan. Nicknamed "Superman" after stopping a penalty kick by Brazilian star Ronaldo in his third season, Gigi was already the league's best goalkeeper when Juventus paid his transfer fee of $61 million in July 2001. He's been with the team ever since.

The biggest thrill of Gigi's career came in 2006 when he led Italy to its first World Cup championship in 24 years. Winning the Yashin Award as the tournament's best keeper, he posted five clean sheets and allowed only two goals—a penalty by France's Zinedine Zidane and an own-goal. Gigi turns 40 in January 2018 and has vowed to retire after the 2017–2018 season—but he does leave open the possibility of return if Juventus wins the Champions League, one of the few titles that's eluded him.

Fast Stat:

974

Consecutive minutes Gigi played in 2015–2016 without conceding a goal, a Serie A record

Ht: 6′3″ • **Wt:** 203 • **DOB:** 1/28/78

Position: Goalkeeper

2017–2018 salary:
$4.7 million

Career club games/International caps:
851 games/173 caps

Twitter: @gianluigibuffon

Did you know? Gigi comes from an athletic family—his mother was a discus thrower and his father a weightlifter, and his two sisters played for the Italian national volleyball team.

As a kid: Gigi idolized Cameroon goalkeeper Thomas N'kono after watching him in the 1990 World Cup.

Fun tidbit: In 2017 Gigi launched his own wine label, called Buffon #1.

Favorite foods: Pasta and a glass of wine, of course, though he's had to cut back as he's gotten older.

Paul Pogba

Hometown: Lagny-sur-Marne, France
Club: Manchester United

4

Number of goals Paul scored with France in 2014, the year of his first World Cup

Ht: 6'2" • **Wt:** 176 • **DOB:** 3/15/93

Position: Midfield

2017–2018 salary:
$19.8 million

Career club goals/International caps:
45 goals/49 caps

Twitter: @paulpogba

Did you know? Paul has twin older brothers, Florentin and Mathias, who also play pro soccer in Europe, but are members of the Guinea national team. Unlike Paul, who was born in France, they were born in Guinea.

As a kid: Paul began his soccer career at the age of six with US Roissy-en-Brie, near his hometown, where he played for seven seasons before moving to US Torcy.

Favorite foods: Pasta with chicken and salmon with potatoes

Hobbies: Travel, playing video games, and watching basketball

Favorite music: Jay Z and Kanye West

Named by the *Guardian* as one of the 10 most promising young players in Europe in January 2014, Paul Pogba has gone on to exceed those lofty expectations. He helped Turin-based Juventus to three straight Serie A league titles and was honored after leading team France to the quarterfinals of the 2014 World Cup as the tournament's Best Young Player. Pogba, nicknamed *Il Polpo Paul* ("Paul the Octopus") and "Pogboom" by Italian fans, is just 23 and promises to become even better. On August 8, 2016, Pogba returned to Manchester United for an all-time record transfer fee of $114.6 million.

Pogba began his youth career in France but showed so much talent he was poached by Manchester United in 2009 at the age of 16, much to the dismay of his former team, Le Havre. After two years on the under-18 team and a frustrating season with the first team, however, Pogba left Man U for Italy and Juventus, where he blossomed. Pogba helped lead Juventus' resurgence, playing with explosive energy and power, able to score goals from almost anywhere on the pitch. In addition to his club's success, Pogba received the Golden Boy award in 2013 (for best under-21 player in Europe) and the Bravo Award in 2014 (best under-21). In 2015 he was named to the 10-man shortlist for the Best Player in Europe Award. Whether it's finding the net from 40 yards out or making mind-boggling moves with the dribble, Pogba has a penchant for the spectacular.

Already a force on France's national team after two years, Pogba said his wish is to compete against his twin older brothers in a match against Guinea.

"People compare us, but where I would win more tackles, Paul is more technically gifted than I ever was... He can be one of the best in the world."

—Patrick Vieira

Pierre-Emerick Aubameyang

Hometown: Laval, France
Club: Borussia Dortmund

Born in France to a father who was a Gabonese team captain and a mother of Spanish descent, Pierre Emerick-Aubameyang began his professional career in Italy, joining A.C. Milan's youth team in 2007. In six matches, Pierre scored against every team he faced, finishing with seven goals and attracting attention from international scouts.

For the next three seasons, Milan loaned Pierre's services to French Ligue 1 teams Dijon, Lille, Monaco, and Saint-Étienne, where he impressed as a speedy young forward. Before the 2011–2012 season, Saint-Étienne signed him to a permanent deal, and Pierre broke out that year, leading Ligue 1 in goals with 16. The next season, he finished second in the league in scoring with 19 goals and led the team to victory in the 2013 Coupe de la Ligue Final.

Having established himself as one of the best players in France, Bundesliga power Borussia Dortmund signed Pierre to a five-year deal in July 2013. In his Bundesliga debut, Pierre scored a hat trick against Augsburg. In 2015, Pierre became the first player in Bundesliga history to score in each of his team's first eight matches of the season. He has led Dortmund in scoring for the last three seasons, from 2014 to 2017, led the league in scoring in 2016–2017, and was named Bundesliga Player of the Year for 2015–2016. In 2016 the *Guardian* named him the eighth best footballer in the world.

Pierre has been the focal point of the Gabon national team since 2009 and a captain since 2015. He led Gabon to the 2012 Africa Cup of Nations quarterfinals.

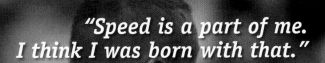

> *"Speed is a part of me.*
> *I think I was born with that."*
>
> —Pierre Emerick-Aubameyang

Fast Stat:

31

Pierre's Bundesliga-leading goal total for 2016–2017

Ht: 6′2″ • **Wt:** 176 • **DOB:** 6/18/89

Position: Forward/Winger

2017–2018 salary:
$5.5 million

Career club goals/International caps:
190 goals/56 caps

Twitter: @Aubameyang7

Did you know? Pierre scored Gabon's first-ever Olympic goal at the 2012 games in London.

Did you know? Both of Pierre's older brothers, Catilina and Willy, played for A.C. Milan's youth team as well.

Fun tidbit: Known for his blazing speed, Pierre ran a 30-meter sprint in 3.7 seconds, faster than Usain Bolt over the same distance.

Favorite foods: His mother's crepes

Interests: Pierre loves Batman and other comic-book superheroes—he once celebrated a DFL-Supercup-clinching goal over Munich by donning a Spider-Man mask.

Favorite music: Hip-hop

Gareth Bale

Hometown: Cardiff, Wales
Club: Real Madrid

Growing up idolizing fellow Welshman pro footballer Ryan Giggs, Gareth Bale was discovered by Southampton at the tender age of nine on his local school team. He made his professional and international debut at the age of 16 in 2006 and was shortly after snapped up by Tottenham Hotspur of the Premier League in 2007.

Though he scored goals against Fulham, Arsenal, and Middlesbrough, Bale endured a winless streak of 24 games across two-plus years to start his tenure with the Spurs, which also saw him suffer a serious injury to his right ankle. After another injury in 2009, Bale returned to the pitch and showed signs of brilliance in his first wins for Tottenham and was named Player of the Month for April 2010.

In 2010–2011 Bale moved from midfield to left wing and became more of an offensive force over the next three seasons, scoring 49 goals.

In 2013 Real Madrid paid a then record transfer fee of £85.3 million to secure Bale's services. Joining Cristiano Ronaldo, Bale contributed key goals in Real Madrid's victories in both the Champions League and Copa del Rey in 2013–2014.

The youngest player to ever score a goal for the Welsh national team, Bale has 54 caps with Wales and 19 goals, making him Wales' sixth-highest scorer of all-time.

One of the fastest players in the world (he could run the 100m in 11.4 seconds at age 14), Bale wears down defenders with his speed and stamina. Also known as a free-kick specialist, Bale's powerful, swerving kicks earned him the nickname "The Cannon" from the Spanish press.

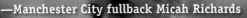

"He made me feel an inch tall. Took me to pieces. He just doesn't stop running. It's ridiculous."

—Manchester City fullback Micah Richards

Fast Stat:

16

Bale's age when he made his professional debut with Southampton in 2006

Ht: 6'0" • **Wt:** 163 • **DOB:** 7/16/89

Position: Midfield/Winger

2017–2018 salary:
$19.7 million

Career club goals/International caps:
130 goals/68 caps

Twitter: @GarethBale11

Did you know? Gareth doesn't drink alcohol. He doesn't care for the taste.

As a kid: During school games, Gareth's coach wouldn't allow him to use his left foot, so as to give the other kids a chance.

Fun tidbit: Gareth had his "heart hands" goal celebration trademarked in 2013.

Favorite foods: Corned beef hash

Hobbies: Hockey, rugby, track & field

Favorite music: Brian McFadden

Eden Hazard

Hometown: Braine-le-Comte, Belgium
Club: Chelsea

As the winner of English soccer's three most prestigious honors in 2014–2015—the PFA Players' Player of the Year, FWA Footballer of the Year, and Premier League Player of the Season—Eden Hazard has conquered British football with Premier League and Football League Cup champion Chelsea. And at the age of 24, he's aiming for the crown currently fought over by Lionel Messi and Cristiano Ronaldo.

The son of Belgian soccer players, Hazard began playing for local clubs in his youth before moving to France to join the club academy at Lille. After two years there, he moved up to the first team at the age of 16. Growing into a key member of the team, he would become the first non-French player to win the UNFP Young Player of the Year award in 2008–2009 and the first man to win the award twice after the next season. For 2010–2011 he became the youngest player to win UNFP Ligue 1 Player of the Year honors, while leading his team to league and Coupe de France titles.

Winning Player of the Year with Lille again in 2011–2012, Hazard then signed with Premier League power Chelsea. In his first season, he helped Chelsea to its first ever UEFA Europa League championship and in 2013–2014 was named the PFA Young Player of the Year before his and his team's explosive 2014–2015 season.

Hazard, who also helped his Belgium national squad to the quarterfinals of the 2014 World Cup, is a deft ball-handler who's been compared to Messi. Hazard is also known for his pace, passing, and technical skills. Already one of the best in the world, Hazard is just getting started.

"On his day, nobody can stop him. He has such great quality on the ball. He can create something from nothing, and this is the sign of a special player."

—Thierry Henry

16

Consecutive penalties Hazard made to start his career—the only European to convert all on 15 or more tries

Ht: 5′8″ • **Wt:** 163 • **DOB:** 1/7/91

Position: Midfield/Winger

2017–2018 salary:
$13.7 million

Career club goals/International caps:
124 goals/80 caps

Twitter: @hazardeden10

Did you know? Eden is a big basketball fan, his favorite player being the New York Knicks' Carmelo Anthony.

As a kid: Eden lived next to a soccer training ground, where he honed his remarkable skills for hours on end.

Favorite foods: Waffles

Hobbies: Dancing, Ping-Pong

Favorite music: Hip-hop, Beyoncé, The Black Eyed Peas, and French gangsta rappers Booba and Gradur

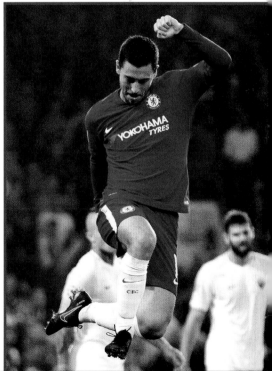

"If you don't live, eat, breathe football, then you're not a true football player. You just wear the jersey."

— Sergio Ramos

Sergio Ramos

Hometown: Camas, Spain
Club: Real Madrid

Captain of both Real Madrid and Spain's national team, Sergio Ramos is considered one of the best big-game players in the world, having led his club to 17 titles and Spain to a World Cup championship in 2010 and European Championships in 2008 and 2012.

Born and raised in Camas, just outside of Sevilla, Sergio has played his entire career in his native Spain. He began his career in the youth system of his local side, Sevilla FC, and made his professional and La Liga debut at the age of 17 in February 2004. Appearing in 41 matches for Sevilla the next season, he helped the team qualify for the UEFA Cup. By the summer of 2005, Real Madrid had taken notice of the speedy, savvy defender and purchased him from Sevilla for $32 million, a record for a Spanish teenager.

Sergio showed a knack for scoring, unusual for defenders, and netted 24 goals in his first four seasons with Madrid. After his 2007–2008 season, Sergio was named to both the UEFA Team of the Year and FIFA's FIFPro World XI, honors he would receive six and five more times, respectively. After scoring in both the semifinal and final of the 2014 FIFA Club World Cup and leading Madrid to victory, he was named the player of the tournament. In 2016 he was named Man of the Match in his second Champions League final, and led Madrid to a third Champions League title in 2017, a season in which he scored a career-high 10 goals.

In the highlight of Sergio's international career, he led Spain to its first World Cup title in 2010, earning top score in the Castrol Performance Index. He looks to lead a talented Spanish team to victory in 2018.

Fast Stat:

20

Number of major club and international titles Sergio has won in his career so far

Ht: 6′0″ • **Wt:** 165 • **DOB:** 3/30/86

Position: Defender

2017–2018 salary: $11.8 million

Career club goals/International caps: 72 club goals/147 caps

Personal homepage: www.sergioramos.com/en

Twitter: @SergioRamos

Did you know? Sergio breeds Andalusian horses on his SR4 stud farm in Sevilla.

As a kid: In Camas, he first played soccer on a field with one goal made by two trees and the other of stones.

Hobbies: Sergio is a fan of bullfighting, popular in his native Andalusia, and is a friend of matador Alejandro Talavante.

Favorite music: Flamenco

Alexis Sánchez

Hometown: Tocopilla, Chile
Club: Arsenal

Known to fans simply as Alexis, this Chilean superstar has found a home with north London's Arsenal, fresh off a 2014–2015 campaign that was the best so far of his already impressive career. After netting his 25th goal in Arsensal's 4–0 FA Cup final victory (a dazzling long-range bender that just grazed the bottom of the crossbar), Alexis was rightfully named the club's Player of the Season, among other honors.

Born and raised in the northern Chilean port of Tocopilla, Alexis was promoted to the Cobreloa first team at the age of 16. He quickly caught the attention of Italian club Udinese, which signed him for a $2.6 million fee in 2006 but immediately loaned him out to Chilean club Colo-Colo for maturation. After breaking into the starting lineup and winning a title there, he played in Argentina for a year. Finally, in 2008 Alexis joined Udinese and spent three seasons in Serie A, once scoring four goals in a match against Palermo in 2011.

His 2011 transfer to Barcelona allowed Alexis to play on a team with some of the best players in the world and to compete for titles in La Liga. Despite nagging injuries in his first season with Barça, he scored 15 goals for a team that won a UEFA Super Cup, Copa del Rey, and a FIFA Club World Cup. A league title followed in 2012–2013, and 2013–2014 saw his top goalscoring production to that point, with 21 goals. It was then Arsenal came calling, and Alexis responded with his breakout season, winning PFA Fans' Player of the Year honors.

A quick, energetic offensive force who can create with either foot, Alexis led his Chilean national team to Copa América titles in both 2015 and 2016.

> *"He's the best signing in the last six years. Arsenal were looking for a player that can deliver on a daily basis—and they have found one."*
>
> —Thierry Henry

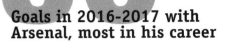

30

Goals in 2016-2017 with Arsenal, most in his career

Ht: 5'7" • **Wt:** 137 • **DOB:** 12/19/88

Position: Winger

2017–2018 salary:
$11.5 million

Career club goals/International caps:
167 goals/118 caps

Twitter: @Alexis_Sanchez

Did you know? His full name is Alexis Alejandro Sánchez Sánchez, but in Chile his nickname is *El Niño Maravilla*, or "The Wonder Boy."

Fun tidbit: Alexis rescued a rabbit (which he later named Alfonso) that had been attacked by a wild boar and nursed it back to health.

As a kid: Alexis played in Cobreloa's youth system, where he was teammates with current national team players Charles Aránguiz and Eduardo Vargas.

Hobbies: Listening to music, browsing the web, social media, and returning home to Chile and his hometown of Tocopilla whenever he can

Favorite music: Niall Horan, Richard Marx, and Latin Pop

"Modric is an outstanding player and in my opinion one of the best midfielders in the world right now."

—Carlo Ancelotti

Luka Modrić

Hometown: Zadar, Croatia
Club: Real Madrid

Forced to flee his home at the age of six when the village of Modrići was captured by Croatian Serb rebels, Luka Modrić started playing soccer in the parking lot at the hotel in Zadar where his family were refugees from the Croatian War of Independence. Began as an escape from a war-torn childhood, Luka's talent soon became apparent, and with help from his extended family, he enrolled in a sporting academy at seven and by the age of 16 joined the youth program of Dinamo Zagreb.

After a season in Zagreb, Dinamo loaned Luka first to a club in the Bosnian Premier League, where he became the Player of the Year at 18, and then to a Croatian side, where he was named Croatian Football Hope of the Year. In 2004 he joined Dinamo's first team and, over the next four seasons led Zagreb to three league titles, two Croatian Cups, and qualification to the UEFA Cup. He was also named Prva HNL Player of the Year in 2007.

The following season, Luka signed with Tottenham Hotspur of the Premier League, where he got off to a slow, injury-plagued start. After a switch back to central/left midfielder, Luka's form improved, as did his team's, culminating in the Spurs' first appearance in the Champions League in almost 50 years. After the 2010–2011 season, Luka was named Tottenham's Player of the Year. By the summer of 2012, Real Madrid came calling and bought Luka's services from the London club for a cool $39 million. Since then Luka has been recognized as one of the best midfielders in the world, winning numerous team and individual honors, including Champions League Best Midfielder 2017 and being named captain of the Croatian national team.

Fast Stat:

5

Number of times Luka has been named the Croatian Footballer of the Year

Ht: 5'9" • **Wt:** 145 • **DOB:** 9/9/85

Position: Midfield

2017–2018 salary:
$8.9 million

Career club goals/International caps:
72 club goals/101 caps

Twitter: @lm19official

Did you know? When asked what he would have become if not for soccer, Luka said, "I would probably have been a barman."

Favorite foods: Italian food

Hobbies: Swimming, playing video games, and watching movies

Favorite music: Shakira, Justin Bieber

Christian Pulisic

Hometown:
Hershey, Pennsylvania
Club: Borussia Dortmund

Having risen faster and higher than any other American player in history, Christian Pulisic is making believers of fans who've waited a long time for a U.S. soccer star to rival those from Europe and Latin America.

Having turned just 18 in September 2016, Pulisic is already a starter on the U.S. soccer squad and a solid contributor on one of Germany's top professional teams, Borussia Dortmund. In April 2016, he became the youngest foreigner to ever score in the Bundesliga, and a week later he became the youngest player of any nationality to score two goals in the league. Still before his 18th birthday, he would also become the youngest player in the modern era to score a goal for the U.S. and then netted two goals in a 2018 World Cup qualification match, making him the youngest American to score a goal in a World Cup Qualifier as well as the youngest to score a brace in U.S. history.

Pulisic grew up in Pennsylvania, the son of a former professional indoor soccer player and coach, and took to the sport at a tender age. After a year spent with a youth team in England at the age of seven, Pulisic played with youth club PA Classics in the Hershey area for seven years before signing with Borussia Dortmund's youth program at the age of 16. In only 15 games with their U19 team, Pulisic scored 10 goals and added another eight assists. Quickly promoted to the first team, he made his Bundesliga debut on January 30, 2016, and started his first match in February. With three more goals in 16 games in 2017–2018, Pulisic finds himself with prospects other American players could only dream of.

Fast Stat:

17

Age at which Christian started for the U.S. national team and Bundesliga power Borussia Dortmund

Ht: 5'8" • **Wt:** 139 • **DOB:** 9/18/98

Position: Midfield/Winger

2017–2018 salary:
$1.1 million

Career club goals/International caps:
10 goals/20 caps

Twitter: @cpulisic_10

Did you know? With a grandfather from Croatia, Christian secured a Croatian passport to avoid having to apply for a work visa after moving to Germany.

Fun Fact: Christian's cousin Will joined Borussia Dortmund's youth team in March 2016.

As a kid: At the age of seven, Christian spent a year in England and played for the youth team of Brackley Town.

Hobbies: Basketball and Ping-Pong

Favorite music: Justin Bieber

"I really think that Pulisic is going to be the best player the United States has ever produced."

—former U.S. U20 coach
Thomas Rongen

Kevin De Bruyne

Hometown: Drongen, Belgium
Club: Manchester City

One of the best young playmakers in soccer today, at 24 Kevin De Bruyne has already made the rounds of European soccer. After an up-and-down early career, he looks to have come into his own, having excelled in Germany with Wolfsburg and now making an impact with Manchester City.

De Bruyne began his youth career at the age of six with KVV Drongen and made his professional debut at 17 with Genk, scoring six goals and 16 assists for a team that won the Belgian Pro League in 2010–2011. His performance there brought interest from Premier League power Chelsea, who brought him over to West London in 2012. Almost immediately, though, he was loaned out to Bundesliga team Werder Bremen for a year before returning to Chelsea in 2013. A combination of Chelsea's already powerful roster and a knee injury in the fall of 2013 limited De Bruyne's appearances, and he was transferred to Wolfsburg in the Bundesliga in January 2014.

In 2014–2015, his breakout season, De Bruyne scored 16 goals and 27 assists in all matches and was named the 2015 Footballer of the Year in Germany. He began the 2015–2016 season by winning the DFL-Supercup against Bayern Munich with an assist and a goal. On August 30, 2015, Manchester City signed De Bruyne for £55 million, one of highest transfer fees in British soccer history. Joining a Man City lineup featuring Kun Agüero and Yaya Touré, De Bruyne netted 16 goals in his first season. A solid contributor on his Belgium national team, De Bruyne scored against the U.S. in the round of 16 at the 2014 World Cup and was named man of the match versus Algeria. A versatile playmaker and goalscorer, De Bruyne has a bright future.

Fast Stat:

27

Assists Kevin made in all matches with Wolfsburg in 2014–2015

Ht: 5'11" • **Wt:** 150 • **DOB:** 6/28/91

Position: Midfield/Winger

2017–2018 salary:
$7.9 million

Career club goals/International caps:
72 goals/53 caps

Twitter: @DeBruyneKev

Did you know? Kevin broke the record for most assists in a Bundesliga season, with 21 in 2014–2015.

As a kid: Kevin played soccer in the garden of the house his parents built in the village of Drongen (part of the city of Ghent) from the age of three until six.

Favorite foods: Cake

Hobbies: Playstation, baking

Favorite music: Electronic dance music, hip-hop, and R&B

"He has that special footballing instinct that not all players have."

—Wolfsburg sporting director
Klaus Allofs

Riyad Mahrez

Hometown: Sarcelles, France
Club: Leicester City

Like many greats, Riyad Mahrez was often overlooked in his youth due to his size. Growing up in the suburbs of Paris, Riyad played soccer on the streets or would sneak into a gym late at night with friends to play. Attributing his thin build to being too busy playing to eat, Riyad joined his local club Sarcelles in 2004 and transferred to fourth-division team Quimper in 2009. After one season he transferred to Le Havre, making the first team and Ligue 2 by the 2012–2013 season, where he made 60 appearances and scored six goals.

While scouting another player on Le Havre for Leicester City, Steve Walsh noticed Riyad instead and offered him a contract. Although Riyad had never heard of them—he thought they were a rugby club—he signed and joined the team in 2014. After Riyad moved up to the first team, Leicester won the EFL Championship league, returning it to the Premier League for the 2014–2015 season. Riyad scored four goals in 30 games that year, as the team narrowly escaped relegation back to the EFL Championship.

Riyad scored a brace in Leicester's 2015–2016 season-opening win, a portent of things to come. It would be a historic season for an underdog team that beat 5,000-to-1 odds to win its first Premier League title, and for Riyad, who would score 18 goals and 11 assists and win the league's Player of the Season award. Although Riyad's numbers dropped off in 2016–2017 with the loss of N'Golo Kanté, he led the team to the quarterfinals of the Champions League, scoring four goals and two assists. Playing for his parents' country of Algeria, Riyad has scored eight goals in 30 caps since debuting for the team in 2014.

Fast Stat:

18

Number of goals Mahrez scored for Leicester City in 2015–2016, second-best on the team

Ht: 5'10" • **Wt:** 134 • **DOB:** 2/21/91

Position: Winger

2017–2018 salary:
$6.9 million

Career club goals/International caps:
71 club goals/30 caps

Twitter: @Mahrez22

Did you know? Riyad's father, who died when Riyad was only 15, had played soccer in Algeria.

Fun tidbit: While with Quimper, Riyad roomed with Mathias Pogba, brother of Man U midfielder Paul Pogba.

As a kid: Riyad said, "As a child… I was always with a ball—that's why I was so skinny, I would miss dinner. Mum would have to leave me some food in the microwave."

Favorite foods: Steak and french fries

Favorite music: Rap

"He's the type of player who enjoys his football.... he wants to play all the time, he's like a kid on the playground."

—former Leicester City manager Craig Shakespeare

Luis Suárez

Hometown: Salto, Uruguay
Club: FC Barcelona

49

Number of goals Suárez has scored in international competition

Ht: 5'11" • **Wt:** 187 • **DOB:** 1/24/87

Position: Striker

2017–2018 salary:
$29.4 million

Career club goals/International caps:
344 club goals/95 caps

Twitter: @LuisSuarez9

Did you know? Luis joined the Groningen club in order to be closer to his childhood sweetheart, Sofia, now his wife, in Barcelona.

As a kid: Luis moved to Montevideo with his family, where he says he really learned to play soccer.

Favorite foods: After biting Giorgio Chiellini at the 2014 World Cup, the joke started on social media that his favorite cuisine was "Italian."

Hobbies: Playing Playstation and spending time with his kids

Favorite music: Latin music

Usually named as one of the top soccer players in the world, Luis Suárez has the distinction of also being recognized as one of the sport's most controversial.

One of eight children, Suárez learned soccer on the streets of the Uruguayan capital of Montevideo, where he also had to work as a street sweeper to help support his family. At the age of 14, Suárez joined the Club Nacional youth team in Montevideo and moved up the ranks to the first team by the time he was 18.

While Dutch club Groningen reps were in Uruguay to scout another player, they saw Suárez play in one game and made an offer to buy him out. Suárez spent one season with Groningen before being bought out by Ajax, where he flourished, scoring 111 goals over four seasons with the Amsterdam club. In 2010 Suárez moved to Liverpool in the Premier League, a £22.8 million signing. In four years there, he netted 82 goals and in 2014 earned the PFA Players' Player of the Year award, Premier League Player of the Year, FWA Footballer of the Year, and shared the European Golden Shoe with Cristiano Ronaldo.

However, Suárez's sometimes questionable tactics have earned him red cards and fan enmity over the years. In the 2010 World Cup he committed a handball in Uruguay's match against Ghana (though it did save the game), and he has bitten three opposing players (the most famous incident occurring in the 2014 World Cup).

Suárez was purchased by Barcelona in 2014 and has scored 126 goals in 162 games for Barça, winning another Golden Shoe in 2015–2016 as La Liga's top scorer.

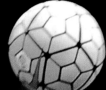

"He is near unplayable. He on his own can occupy a back four with his movement and his cleverness."

—Liverpool manager Brendan Rodgers

FIFA World Cup

Presenting the FIFA World Cup trophy in Moscow's Luzhniki Stadium

Russia 2018

FIFA WORLD CUP RUSSIA 2018

HOW IT WORKS

Winnowing the World's Teams Down to 32

With more than 200 teams around the world vying to qualify for the World Cup every four years, FIFA, the international governing body for association soccer, has developed an intricate system for teams to play their way in. For the 2018 World Cup, the process began not long after the 2014 World Cup ended. And for the first time ever, every eligible team (except for host Russia) participated in the 868 matches played in the qualifying tournaments.

In international soccer, FIFA divides the world into six regions overseen by their respective confederations: Europe (UEFA), South America (CONMEBOL), Africa (CAF), Asia (AFC), North/Central America and the Caribbean (CONCACAF), and Oceania, or the Pacific Islands (OFC).

European teams were sorted into nine groups of six teams, from which 14 teams would ultimately qualify for the field of 32. Russia, as the host, qualified automatically. Round 1 saw teams play 10 home-and-away matches from September 2016 to October 2017. The winners of the nine groups—determined by record and any ties broken by point differential—qualified for the World Cup. The eight best second-place teams then had to play second-round matches in November 2017, from which the four winners qualified for the 2018 World Cup.

Africa held three elimination rounds for its 53 teams, starting in October 2015 and finishing in November 2017, from which five group winners would qualify.

The 10 South American teams played from October 2015 to October 2017, the four best qualifying for Russia. The fifth-place team from South America advanced to a home-and-away playoff with the winner of the Oceania tournament. The best of Oceania's 11 teams would only make it to the World Cup if they won the playoff.

North/Central America and the Caribbean got three guaranteed spots out of 35 teams, which played five rounds from March 2015 to October 2017. Asia got four out of 46 teams after three rounds and a playoff played over the same period. One team from each region competed in two playoff games in November 2017 to determine the remaining spot in the World Cup.

After the 32 teams were determined, a draw, held in Moscow on December 1, 2017, sorted the 32 teams into eight groups of four.

Luzhniki Stadium, Moscow

THE FIELD

The 32 Teams from Their Respective Regions

Africa (CAF):
- Egypt
- Morocco
- Nigeria
- Senegal
- Tunisia

Asia (AFC):
- Australia
- Iran
- Japan
- Saudi Arabia
- South Korea

Europe (UEFA):
- Belgium
- Croatia
- Denmark
- England
- France
- Germany
- Iceland
- Poland
- Portugal
- Russia
- Serbia
- Spain
- Sweden
- Switzerland

North/Central America & Caribbean (CONCACAF):
- Costa Rica
- Mexico
- Panama

South America (CONMEBOL):
- Argentina
- Brazil
- Colombia
- Peru
- Uruguay

Russia 2018

The Games—from Group Play to the Final

The 32 teams, once sorted into eight groups (A–H), are seeded by their FIFA ranking (except for Russia, which as host, gets an automatic No. 1 seed).

The 21st FIFA World Cup begins on June 14, 2018, with host Russia facing the second seed from the A group in Moscow. Over the next 14 days, three to four group matches will take place every day to determine the top two teams from each group. Starting on June 30, the Round of 16 games begin to narrow the field down to eight. The quarterfinals start on July 6. The winners of those four matches will meet in the semifinals on July 10 and 11 in Saint Petersburg and Moscow to determine the finalists. After a third-place match played in Saint Petersburg on July 14, the World Cup Final will be played in Luzhniki Stadium in Moscow on Sunday, July 15, 2018, at 6:00 PM local time.

Twelve different venues across Russia will host group matches from June 14–28: Ekaterinburg Arena, Kaliningrad Stadium, Kazan Arena, Luzhniki Stadium (Moscow), Spartak Stadium (Moscow), Nizhny Novgorod Stadium, Rostov Arena (Rostov-on-Don), Saint Petersburg Stadium, Samara Arena, Mordovia Arena (Saransk), Fisht Stadium (Sochi), and Volgograd Arena. Two Round of 16 matches will take place each day from June 30 to July 3 in eight of the venues. Four quarterfinal matches will be played over two days, July 6–7, in four of the venues, culminating in the semifinals and World Cup Final in Saint Petersburg Stadium and Moscow's upgraded, 81,000-seat Luzhniki Stadium.

The Top 10

GERMANY

The reigning World Cup champions from 2014 look to be the first team to repeat as winners since Brazil did it in 1958 and 1962. With a lineup that boasts weapons like Thomas Müller and Mesut Özil and a defense that includes Toni Kroos, Mats Hummels, and one of the best goalkeepers in the world, Manuel Neuer, Germany is in a great position to do just that. Having won their qualifying group with a 10–0 record, Germany's defense allowed only two goals, similar to the way it allowed just one goal during its World Cup 2014 championship run—and that only came at the end of their 7–1 rout of host Brazil.

World Cup titles: **4** (3 as West Germany) **Apps:** **18**

Players to watch: Mesut Özil, Toni Kroos, Thomas Müller, Mats Hummels, Manuel Neuer, Mario Götze

BRAZIL

After its humiliating 7–1 loss in the 2014 World Cup to Germany on its home turf, Brazil is determined to climb back to the top of international soccer. They dominated their group with a 12–1–5 record, their last loss coming in the first qualifier played against Chile back in 2015. With a new coach, Tite, and rediscovered swagger, Brazil became the first team to qualify for the 2018 World Cup with a 3–0 defeat of Paraguay in March 2017. That's good news for a country that eats, sleeps, and breathes football. With Neymar, one of the greatest goalscorers in the world after Messi and Ronaldo, Brazil is hoping to ride him and a deep roster of all-stars to their sixth World Cup championship.

World Cup titles: 5 **Apps:** 20

Players to watch: Neymar, Paulinho, Gabriel Jesus, Douglas Costa, Philippe Coutinho

SPAIN

Home to the world's preeminent professional league, La Liga, which boasts the world's two greatest players and a few others who make the top 10 (the recent departure of Neymar notwithstanding), Spain is also home to some pretty impressive local talent. The Spanish national team went undefeated in its group stage, scoring 36 goals in 10 matches with only three against. With star midfielders like Sergio Ramos and Andrés Iniesta (who scored the game-winning goal to give Spain its first World Cup in 2010), *La Roja* employs a style that's been dubbed "tiki-taka," a game that emphasizes short passing, patience, technique, and possession above all. Despite club affiliations that carry intense rivalries (think Ramos' Real Madrid versus Iniesta's FC Barcelona), when the players come together for Spain, they leave the rest behind and play as one unified team. A mix of experience and young talent will make them hard to beat.

World Cup titles: 1 **Apps:** 14

Players to watch: Sergio Ramos, Andrés Iniesta, Pedro, Gerard Piqué, Sergio Busquets, David Silva, Álvaro Morata

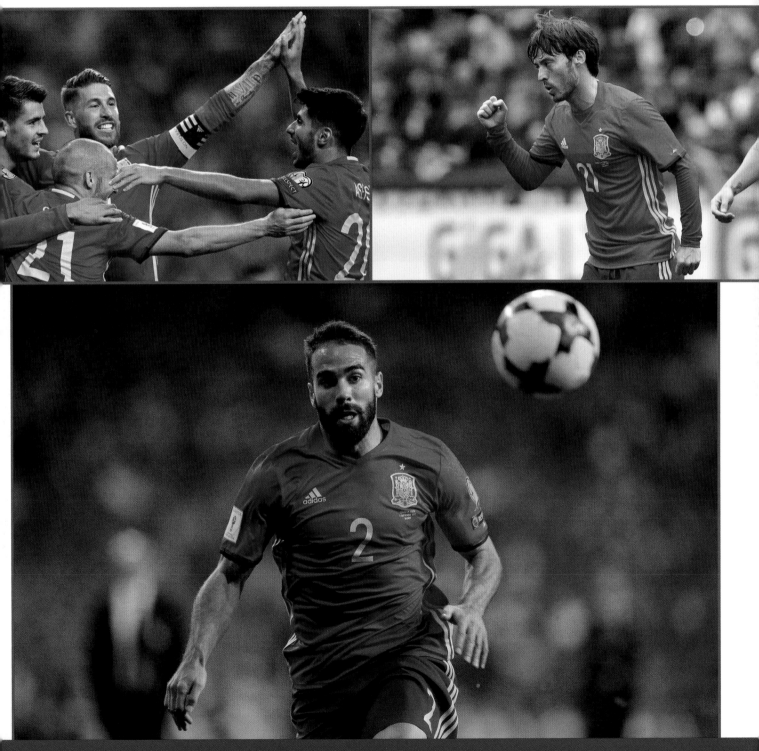

PORTUGAL

Cristiano Ronaldo's national team beat out Switzerland in group competition, despite owning an identical 9–0–1 record, by hammering its opponents with a 32–4 goal margin. In 2016 it won the UEFA Euro—its first major title ever—by going through Poland and Wales and then beating France 1–0 on their home field. Built around Ronaldo, one of the twin pillars of modern soccer, Portugal is solid on defense with the veteran Pepe and the young midfielder Raphaël Guerreiro. With a seasoned goalkeeper in Rui Patrício, Portugal is tough to score on, as its group opponents learned. With Ronaldo, a nightmare for defenses who can score anytime from just about anywhere on the pitch, and a young scoring threat in André Silva, the Portuguese team is an offensive force as well. Portugal has put together a side to match the player often considered the best in the world and is looking to add a second major title to its name—the World Cup.

World Cup titles: 0 **Apps:** 6

Players to watch: Cristiano Ronaldo, Renato Sanches, Rui Patrício, André Silva

ARGENTINA

Having appeared in five World Cup finals—including the first in 1930 and most recent in 2014—and claiming gold in the 2008 Olympics, Argentina boasts one of the most intimidating traditions in international soccer. Add to that arguably the greatest goalscorer of his generation in Lionel Messi and one of the best strikers in the world in Sergio Agüero, and *La Albiceleste* has to be considered a strong contender in 2018. After losing a heartbreaking final to Germany in 2014 in Brazil, Argentina struggled, losing the Copa América Centenario in 2016 and enduring a brief retirement from international play by Messi. With Messi's return and a new coach in Jorge Sampaoli, Argentina has begun to play the kind of soccer that could return them to the final and earn Messi the one title that's so far eluded him.

World Cup titles: 2 **Apps:** 16

Players to watch: Lionel Messi, Sergio Agüero, Ángel Di María, Sergio Romero

COLOMBIA

The people of Colombia take a special pride in their national team, *Los Cafeteros*. After great success in the 1990s, they suffered through a 16-year absence from the World Cup. But in 2014 coach José Pékerman led Colombia back to the tournament in Brazil, taking the team all the way to the quarterfinals for the first time in its history. In the 2014 World Cup, 23-year-old James Rodríguez emerged as an international star, leading the tournament in scoring with six goals and winning the Golden Boot, while teammate Juan Cuadrado paced the field with the most assists. Rodríguez will turn 27 during the 2018 World Cup and will lead a Colombia team loaded with young talent and experience playing in the most competitive professional leagues in the world.

World Cup titles: 0 **Apps:** 5

Players to watch: James Rodríguez, Radamel Falcao, Jua Cuadrado, David Ospina

FRANCE

Perhaps no team other than Germany can boast as many superstars on one roster as France. Antoine Griezmann, Paul Pogba, and N'Golo Kanté would seem to be an unstoppable trio. Yet *Les blues* are coming off a disappointing loss to Portugal in the Euro 2016 final and did not exactly dominate en route to finishing first in their group. Coach Didier Deschamps has been criticized for his decision-making, and his most difficult choice in the World Cup may be choosing which players to employ from such a deep bench. An easy decision will be who to play in goal, as French captain Hugo Lloris is one of the best in the world. A three-time Ligue 1 Goalkeeper of the Year with Lyon, Lloris posted five clean sheets during France's group stage, including two over ousted Netherlands. If the team gets hot in Russia this summer, they have the talent to go all the way and capture their second World Cup.

World Cup titles: 1   Apps: 14

Players to watch: Antoine Griezmann, Paul Pogba, N'Golo Kanté, Olivier Giroud, Kylian Mbappe, Hugo Lloris

PERU

The Peruvian team hasn't qualified for the World Cup since 1982, at the end of the team's decade-long resurgence in the 1970s. After Argentina ended its World Cup–qualifying hopes in 1986, Peru has struggled to rediscover its mojo. Former Argentinian national player Ricardo Gareca—whose goal ended Peru's World Cup chances in '86—took over as *Los Incas* coach in 2015 and has led a resurgence of a proud team looking to emerge from South America, one of the toughest regions in the world to compete in soccer. Finishing fifth in the CONMEBOL group stage, Peru shut out New Zealand 2–0 on aggregate in a home-and-away playoff to secure its place in Russia. With veteran forwards Paolo Guerrero and Jefferson Farfán and a wealth of young talent, Peru is on the way up after finishing third at the 2015 Copa América and reaching the quarterfinals of the Copa América Centenario. Although not a favorite to win, Peruvian fans hope 2018 will be the year the White and Red return to glory.

World Cup titles? 0 **Apps:** 4

Players to watch: Paolo Guerrero, Jefferson Farfán, Christian Cueva, André Carrillo

BELGIUM

With scoring stars like Eden Hazard, Kevin De Bruyne, and Romelu Lukaku, and a stingy young goalkeeper in Thibaut Courtois, Belgium won its qualifying group handily, posting a 9–0–1 record while outscoring its opponents 43–6. Despite its small size (just over 10 million people), Belgium has produced some of the world's greatest soccer talent in recent years, topping the FIFA World Rankings for the first time in November 2015. Qualifying for its 13th World Cup since 1930, the *Diables Rouges* (Red Devils) have never advanced beyond the semifinals in World Cup play, which they did back in 1986. But with a team this talented and young, Belgium has to be one of the favorites, even against the likes of Germany and Brazil. Taking over the team in 2016, Roberto Martínez added French legend Thierry Henry to his coaching staff, as Belgium hopes that in 2018 it can go further than it's ever gone in the World Cup before.

World Cup titles: 0 **Apps:** 12

Players to watch: Eden Hazard, Kevin de Bruyne, Romelu Lukaku, Thibaut Courtois, Thomas Meunier

POLAND

Making the World Cup for the first time since 2006, Poland won their group easily, going 8–1 and earning a ticket to Russia with a 4–2 defeat of Montenegro. With a core group of players who mostly play abroad, Poland fields a stronger team than they've had in decades. After missing the last World Cup, they atoned by beating World Cup champion Germany for the first time ever in October 2014 by a score of 2–0. With captain Robert Lewandowski—the reigning Bundesliga Player of the Year—leading all scorers in the 2018 World Cup qualification stage with 16, Poland possesses one of the top strikers in the world. Experienced winger Jakub Blaszczykowski, defensive stand-out Grzegorz Krychowiak, and top-class goalkeeper Wojciech Szczesny give Poland good reason for hope in 2018.

World Cup titles: 0 **Apps:** 7

Players to watch: Robert Lewandowski, Wojciech Szczęsny, Jakub Błaszczykowski, Grzegorz Krychowiak

Other Teams to Keep an Eye On

ENGLAND Making its sixth straight World Cup, the English haven't won it all since 1966. But a talented crop of young players make the Three Lions hard to beat.

SWITZERLAND In their 11th World Cup, the Swiss have yet to win one. But the teenagers who won the 2009 U-17 World Cup are now in their prime and will pose a challenge for any team that draws them.

URUGUAY Second behind Brazil and ahead of Argentina in its CONMEBOL group, Uruguay has Luis Suárez, striker Edinson Cavani, and a proud history that includes two World Cup trophies.

MEXICO With the fourth most appearances in the World Cup (15), Mexico finished first among all teams in the group stage in North/Central America and the Caribbean.

CROATIA Edged out by Iceland in its group, Croatia is led by captain Luka Modrić and fellow playmaker Ivan Rakitić, two of the best players in the world.

ICELAND Coming off a victory over England in Euro 2016, Iceland won its group to qualify for its first-ever World Cup berth—the smallest country by population to ever make it in, a true underdog and a sentimental favorite.

SWEDEN Defeating Italy in the playoff round by blanking the Italians twice, Sweden qualified for its 12th World Cup and hopes to go further than the round of 16.

SENEGAL The team outside of Europe or Latin America with the best chance of advancing, Senegal made it to the quarterfinals in the 2002 World Cup.

England

Croatia

U.S.A.

Epic Fails

CHILE Ranked among the top 10 teams by FIFA, Chile couldn't finish among the top five in its CONMEBOL group, getting edged out by Peru.

ITALY Tied for the second-most World Cup championships with four, Italy failed to score a goal against Sweden in two playoff games, losing 1–0 on aggregate.

U.S.A. Even after Panama and Honduras won, U.S.A. only needed to tie 1–8 Trinidad and Tobago to qualify for its eighth consecutive World Cup. Final score: Trinidad 2, U.S.A. 1.

Cristiano Ronaldo

Luka Modrić

I had to admit that I was feeling pretty flattered about being chosen for Miss Keller's writing class . . . but there were all those rumors about her. Like, she had an evil temper, held grudges, and took a deep and abiding personal dislike to some of her students, and that in her entire career, she had never given a student an A.

Everyone called her Killer Keller. Even other teachers.

Patricia Lee Gauch, Editor

No part of this publication may be
reproduced, stored in a retrieval system,
or transmitted in any form or by any
means, electronic, mechanical,
photocopying, recording, or otherwise,
without written permission of the publisher.
For information regarding permission,
write to G. P. Putnam's Sons, an imprint
of Penguin Young Readers Group,
a division of Penguin Random House LLC,
375 Hudson Street, New York, NY 10014.

ISBN 978-1-338-12045-5

Copyright © 2015 by Patricia Polacco.
All rights reserved. Published by Scholastic
Inc., 557 Broadway, New York, NY 10012,
by arrangement with G. P. Putnam's Sons,
an imprint of Penguin Young Readers Group,
a division of Penguin Random House LLC.
SCHOLASTIC and associated logos are
trademarks and/or registered trademarks of
Scholastic Inc.

The publisher does not have any control
over and does not assume any responsibility
for author or third-party websites or their
content.

12 11 10 9 8 7 6 5 4 3 2 1   16 17 18 19 20 21

Printed in the U.S.A.   40

First Scholastic printing, September 2016

Design by Siobhán Gallagher
Text set in Garth Graphic Std
The illustrations are rendered in
pencils and markers.

an Ⓐ from Miss Keller

Patricia Polacco

SCHOLASTIC INC.

On the first day of class, Miss Keller slithered into the room, and strutting up and down the aisles, snarled, "I am going to transform each and every one of you into a crackerjack writer! One enormous miracle, right?

"But," she barked in a deep Southern accent, "if you think this class is going to be simple, head for the door right now. You are going to work harder than you have ever worked in your entire miserable little lives. Some of you may not make it through the term!"

I felt as if she was looking right at me.

Miss Keller seemed taller than she really was. She stood stiff and erect, but when she was at her desk, she reminded me of a bird of prey perched on a dead limb, ready to swoop down on one of us.

"Your first assignment is going to be an essay. I expect you to dazzle me. Impress me. Send me into ecstasy with your brilliance.

"I want to see if you deserve to be here at all! The subject? Your families and your home life—the inside story." We all scrambled, took out paper, and started to write.

"No, no! Not in class!" she boomed. We all dropped our pencils. "This is a homework assignment. Three full pages and no grammatical errors. Due tomorrow!"

I swallowed hard.

The whole way home, all I could think about was that essay. It just had to be good!

I turned up the hill and walked toward my house. Pop Schloss, our next-door neighbor, was sitting on his front steps. He lived alone, wife gone, kids grown. He patted the step next to him.

"Bad day?" he asked, pulling a bag from his pocket and offering me a newly baked cookie. Pop, known far and wide for being a master pastry chef, always carried cookies in his pocket.

"I have the meanest teacher in the whole school!"

"Not Killer Keller?" Pop pretended to hold his head in shock. I nodded. "Hmmm. Both of my sons had her in school. Remind me to tell you a story about her sometime."

We both just sat and watched the birds land on the telephone wire across the street. Like I said, that essay had to be good.

That night, I took to my desk and began to write. I loved my room, and it was a big part of my home life, so I looked around and began to describe it. In detail! I wrote about how I loved my cat, my mom, my new skirt, eating breakfast—I felt masterful. This was, I thought, some of the best writing I had ever done.

I could hardly wait to read it out loud in class.

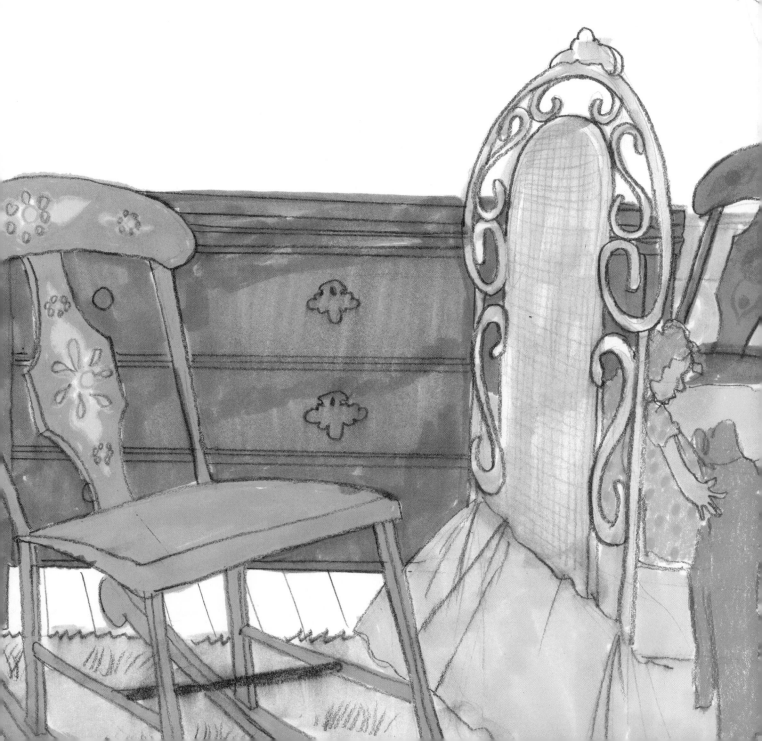

The next morning, one by one, my classmates read their essays out loud. I wasn't afraid to read, but I was sure nervous. Then I heard my name.

"Miss Barber, you're next."

I read my masterpiece about my family, my home life, about how I loved everyone and everything about it. I was sure Miss Keller would be impressed, but she started pacing.

"Miss Barber, you used the word *love* to describe your cat, your skirt, your neighbor, a pile of pancakes . . . and your mother. Do you feel the same about a plate of pancakes as you do your mother? Words convey feelings. But there are differences!

"Class, take out a piece of paper and make a list of words that convey love. But . . . *love* is the one word you cannot use."

We all tried, but our lists were very, very short.

"All right, class." She swept to the front of the room. "Do you know what a thesaurus is? And no, it is not a prehistoric lizard!" No one could answer. "That is your assignment for tonight. Figure it out, bring a thesaurus to class, and look up the word *love*."

After I got home that afternoon, I ran next door to see Pop.

"A thesaurus? I think I still have mine that the boys used when they had Miss Keller," he bubbled as he trundled into their old room.

"And yes siree, here it is!" He pulled out a small paperback from a pile of books. "All the words are listed in alphabetical order. And in the back? Word choices—over 150,000. If I remember Miss Keller, this book will be your bible from now on."

That very next day, Miss Keller wrote a list of words on the board—*content*, *cool*, *loyal*—and told us to use our thesaurus to list as many alternatives to each word as we could find. Whoever got the longest lists would be excused from the Friday quiz.

Guess what? I had the longest lists! I had actually done something right! No quiz. But out at recess Eric Yangden and Tim Farkus started teasing, "Looks like the dumbbell is teacher's new pet!"

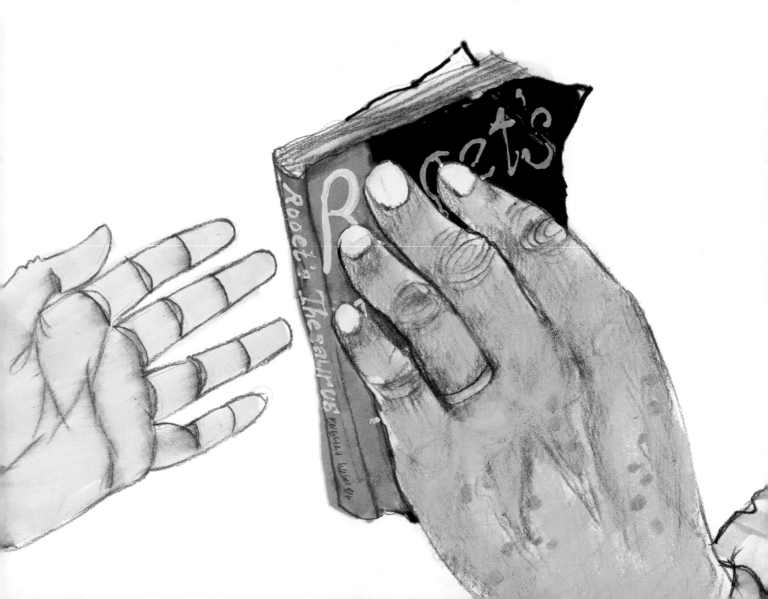

As the days passed, Miss Keller gave our class all kinds of writing exercises to do. Sometimes in the classroom, sometimes out. We went outside one day to listen to trees—to sharpen our senses, Miss Keller said. We listened in on conversations in the lunchroom for a dialogue assignment. To begin to understand color, we went to the town dump!

One day, she brought a bunch of objects right into the classroom—handlebars, a screwdriver, a cup—set them out, and told us, "Look at each object and make a list of what we could use them for, except for the use they were meant for."

For homework that night, she asked us to interview an older person about an object in his or her house that meant something to him or her—a pretty dish or tablecloth, a figurine. She called it a "found object."

Of course I knew exactly whom I was going to interview.

Pop!

Pop and I walked around his house together. "What are you going to pick as your 'found object,' Pop?" I asked. He just couldn't seem to decide. After a time, he walked over to his mantel and took down a beautiful photograph.

"This lovely woman is my Millie. I was in love with her from the first moment I laid eyes on her," he whispered quietly. "She was so lovely, Patricia. When she walked into a room, the sun and moon would peek into the window just to get a glimpse of her. Oh, how I miss her," his voice trailed off.

He talked to me about his Millie for the next hour. I started writing before I left his house.

I was sure I nailed it this time. I wrote with oodles of heart and feeling. I couldn't wait for Miss Keller to see this essay. But when she handed it back, there was a C scrawled at the bottom. Again.

What did she want from me anyway? She kept me after school that day.

"Miss Barber, your paper on your neighbor's Millie was, well, adequate. But where are the words that truly show emotion?" Then she turned and looked right at me. "The reader needs to FEEL what you feel, Miss Barber, but not in an ordinary way. Be daring, unexpected, surprising . . . original!"

Now she gazed deeply into my eyes. "You have the words, Patricia. You have to give them wings!"

That day I found Pop out in his backyard feeding his koi fish in the pond. Pop could see I was upset.

I told him everything. That the boys in class were still calling me "teacher's pet" even though Miss Keller was harder on me than anyone. That today she'd said I lacked emotional connection in my writing.

"My guess is old Killer Keller has taken a real interest in you, or she would have just let you sit there like a bump on a log. As for the teasing, do you know what my first name is? It's Lynn. The guys in my class loved that, and I was the only boy in the cooking class, too. They never let me live that down, either!"

The two of us laughed so hard, we could hardly catch our breath. I had noticed before that Pop sometimes took pills. He said they were "to keep his ticker going." I knew that meant his heart. Today I noticed he slipped two pills under his tongue.

Days with Miss Keller seemed to fly by—none of them easy for me.

Then one day, she called us together. "Today, I am assigning you the dreaded term essay!" I'd heard about it, all right! "I have taught you many forms of writing: dialogue and scene, opinion essay, personal narrative . . . choose one of these for this last big assignment, and choose well. The grade I give you may well determine if you pass!"

I was already sweating. To make things worse, she asked me to stay after "for a little chat."

"Patricia," she said, "I hope you choose a personal narrative, because quite frankly your writing still lacks emotional connection with the reader."

But no matter how hard I tried, I couldn't come up with a subject for my term essay emotional enough for Miss Keller.

The last Sunday before my deadline to hand in the topic, all of us kids—Stewart, Winnie, Chantille—were at Pop's baking cookies for a block party to help raise money for Mrs. Scudder across the street. She had fallen down her back stairs and broken bones.

As we were rolling the cookies out, Stewart asked me how I liked Miss Keller. I told him that no matter what I did, no matter what I wrote, it didn't seem to please her. "To top it all off," I said, "tomorrow our topic is due for the term essay, and I don't have one!"

"That reminds me! I told you that I'd tell you a story about Miss Keller," Pop said thoughtfully as he rolled out a ball of cookie dough. "All of you kids know she is one tough teacher. But not too long ago she came across one of the most talented writers she'd seen. She picked apart everything he wrote, had him do it over—and over—until he got it right.

"Truth is, he'd never worked so hard for a teacher in his life."

"So what happened to that kid, Pop?" Stewart asked.

"Well, he became a writer. Went to work for the biggest newspaper in Chicago! Then to the biggest paper in Washington, DC. He covered stories from South America to the Middle East to Soviet Russia. Once, he won a Pulitzer Prize for reporting."

"He probably would have gone on to do that anyway, Miss Keller or not."

"Not really, Trisha. This boy's family could never have afforded to send him to college. Miss Keller not only taught him how to write, she raised money for his tuition and fees and personally saw to it that he attended journalism school. Otherwise, he might have ended up working in his father's bakery," Pop said with a glint in his eye.

"That's right. That kid was my very own son . . . and I, for one, am grateful for that dogged high-spirited woman! Killer Keller. Without her, well, who knows . . ."

He slipped another pill under his tongue.

Not a week later—still with no essay topic—I'd come early to Miss Keller's class when the office secretary came in and gave a note to her. "Miss Barber," Miss Keller said. "We need to go to the office." She looked shocked and sad.

When we got to the office, my mother was there. I could see she had been crying. She told me Pop had passed away that morning. A sudden heart attack.

As we pulled into our garage, I saw Pop's sons. They looked so heartbroken. All I wanted was to go through his house one last time. His sons invited me over. I walked through every room. Touched his pillow on his bed. Ran my hand across the back of his favorite chair. Held his bakery coat that he wore when we helped him make cookies. I couldn't stop crying. The sky wasn't happy anymore. How could the earth still be turning when someone like Pop had left it.

That night, I sat at my desk and started writing. I wrote and wrote and wrote.

It seemed like the whole neighborhood was at Pop's funeral. Even Miss Keller. And the shops on College Avenue closed for the day. Everything looked different somehow. My sadness hurt everywhere.

Long after it was due, I placed the piece I had written the day Pop died on Miss Keller's desk. I didn't really care anymore whether I impressed her or not. All that mattered was how I felt about him.

A few days later, I got a pink slip from Miss Keller to come and see her. My heart almost stopped. Anyone who got a pink slip was about to get real bad news because it was the end of the term. She must have hated my essay!

I started sobbing. First Pop, now this. I didn't even know if I would pass.

But when I walked into her room, she actually took both my hands. "Patricia dear, I am so sorry for your loss," she said. Then I saw my essay folded in half on her desk.

"I have graded your essay," she began. "I don't want you to unfold it until you are home, do you understand?" I shook my head yes.

Then she did something that startled me. She hugged me. She actually hugged me!

Then she whispered, "Patricia, you wrote a stunning tribute to Pop. The crowning example of a personal narrative."

My heart sang as I ran all the way home with my essay still folded in my hand.

As I climbed the hill, I stopped and looked up at Pop's house for a moment.

"You're with Millie now, Pop!" I whispered. That thought made me warm inside.

Then I opened my folded paper. There, written in red across the top of the cover sheet: "Patricia, your spelling still leaves much to be desired; however, you've given your words wings! I am departing from my custom . . . here is your A."

My heart warms whenever I think of Miss Keller. She later told me that she was impressed with how I used Pop's very own thesaurus to write my papers. I remember his notes were in the margins in his own handwriting. When I read them, it seemed to bring me closer to him.

Certainly, I did use the word "love." However, I used every form of it. To this day, when I think of Pop and Miss Keller, my thoughts soar, for I shall always regard them as "beloved."

Patricia Polacco